GENERAL GROWTH OF SMEs

Growth of SMEs is basically a stage which needs substantial cash support for the growth project. SMEs all over the world are facing financing problems. Banks found SMEs financing risky and SMEs are not able to gain their financing from banks.

This is not a dead end. SMEs can search for angel financing with a financing rule in exchange for shareholding rights. This is fair and square but if SMEs do not want to have not well known partners, SMEs could see to their bad debts in the company.

Companies should have provided credit terms to customers for example Net 30 (30 days credit). Companies can try to increase customer's credit terms to Net 90 (90 days credit) and see if they could pay for your companies' service. Should companies be not able to get back the payments, bad debts increase in your company. Here comes the account - Provision for bad debts. If so, SMEs could find for example Dun & Bradstreet to help in bad debts collection in exchange of a certain percentage to the bad debts collection firm. Through this firm, SMEs could see their customers' background as well by buying their companies' report for knowing more about their customers if they are a firm. After this stage, one could let go the provision and list the customers' payment as bad debt expenses.

In search for growth in SMEs, SMEs could see if they could be able to join together as a union or association and ask for taxation reduction from the government. With tax reduction, there could be more cash in hand for growth as well as reduce the burden of SMEs during their maturity and decline stage with which SMEs have to face a lot of challenges in these two stages. This could be a plan for SMEs as government needs time to support SMEs through tax reduction (as in China) and if it is successful, SMEs could possibly be able to be supported by the government and face challenges in the maturity and decline stages.

SMEs could think of IPO (Initial Public Offering) as well, as mentioned in my previous talk on survival of SMEs. It can be found at amazon.com titled The Handbook: 12 days rescue for the survival of SMEs (Small and Medium Enterprises).

RETAIL INDUSTRY

The survival of SMEs is basically firstly important for the business life cycle - Infant stage and decline stage. Whether you can reach the growth stage depends greatly on the infant stage. There are five stages in the business life cycle and they are infant stage, growth stage, maturity stage, decline stage and rejuvenation stage **(Kotler)**.

Now I will be concentrating in providing issues for the growth of different industries and the first industry will be retail industry.

During the infant stage, SMEs should be able to sell moderately and have reached or passed basically breakeven and/or above with stability in their businesses. With this, SMEs should be having a number of returned customers with respect to their product sales. This basically means SMEs in this stage can manage their revenue for a jump to the growth stage of the businesses. Hereby we reach an old topic from my previous book - cash management of excessive cash.

Small businesses can head towards online sales and open their market to the world. The cost of getting online is not substantial with which simply launching a web-site through the internet will be suitable. Design and promotion of the web-site will be needed and this cost cash spending to reach the goal of opening the business to the world. Credit card payment method should be included on the web-site and basically it is free with the credit card service from banks and needs only to pay back certain percentage if there is credit card sale. Mind your inventory control and make sure that there is enough inventory and not excessive inventory in your businesses or else there might be heavy cash outflow and might lead to failure in this stage. Inventory control could be managed with a well-established computerized accounting system. How a product sells in the business can be checked from the system. With this, you can manage your inventory with which you can find which product is best seller and which products need to manage to prevent excessive inventory in your store.

Medium businesses can search for other spot to expand their businesses. Hereby refers to place like Thailand as mentioned in my previous talk in the survival of SMEs. Cost control is the key. Do not expand with excessive spending even though you have excessive cash. Diversification as mentioned before in the survival of SMEs might be needed so as to reduce risk in the businesses. Make sure that the businesses at present can support the new spot and the new spot has to pass the infant stage as well during the growth stage of the mother businesses.

Both small and medium businesses could expand their product lines in their product sales. This will lead to additional attractiveness in the business and generating more customers to support the growth stage. This is what I mentioned in my previous talk one of the component of 4P's (E.Jerome McCarthy 1960) - product.

Should you wish to know what I mentioned in my previous talks, you can find them in the published handbook mentioned above.

Next talk will be wholesale industry and I would like to mention again: establish a healthy and detailed computerized accounting system for your businesses and it can help you to manage well your entities if you wish to go to the stage of growth.

Next stop is wholesale industry.

WHOLESALE INDUSTRY

Hereby I will be introducing growth in wholesale industry. Wholesale industry wins through bulk selling. It sells to retail stores for profits.

Wholesale industry can sell products to supermarkets as well. Supermarkets have promotion shelf with which choosing the right place to place your products to sell in supermarkets can help in selling. Supermarkets charge wholesalers a price of promotion on shelf or at road side of the supermarkets. Therefore, SMEs need to control the price of the products to be sold in supermarkets. Usually special discount for supermarkets can help in selling and allow supermarkets to take your products to sell in their place.

SMEs in wholesaling have to control the retail price of products to standardize its profits. Besides, wholesale SMEs should price their products through the standard of expiry date. The nearer the expiry date and less SMEs should earn and can sell at special discount to retailers and even at cost to sell in bulk to retailers once it reaches a stage that the products are going to expire.

Wholesale SMEs can set up a wholesale outlet at times to sell your products. Make sure that the pricing of the products does not compete with your retailers.

Have close relationship with your retailers. Check out the selling behaviour and numbers of products from retailers and you can help in your own ordering, if not, there will be substantial inventory that occupies your profit margin.

Next will be service industry.

SERVICE INDUSTRY

This will be talking about service industry and what can owners do to build up the growth of service industry SMEs.

Service industry includes a lot of different businesses which are IT, Recruiting, Law firm, Clinic, Consulting firm, Accounting firm, Marketing companies and lots more. All of these kinds of businesses are customer oriented.

Service SMEs can collaborate with other companies in other countries and or local through joint venture for their growth in their businesses. SMEs need not set up a subsidiary but head for collaborators to provide their services and accept new businesses from outside the country or from local collaborator through joint venture. With this, service SMEs can provide services to their present customers and new customers should they have other businesses from other country and or the local collaborators. Through joint venture, one can extend their businesses to new markets. How can one search for collaborators to extend their businesses in other markets and or local? SMEs could go for International fairs to find collaborators and reach their growth goal. At this moment, SMEs should have excessive cash in hand for a joint venture project with other companies.

Pricing in service industry is very important. The price of a job could be calculated by manpower hour. SMEs could calculate by taking the total manpower payment of the company through using their salaries per hour, and then electricity, telephone, fax and internet expenses and rental fee (if any) per hour (major expenses) as basis. This calculates a basis of how much is the cost per hour. Then SMEs could add in certain profit margin to the figure and basically set their service price through people orientation. With this figure, one has to multiply with the total job hours to finish the job and should include miscellaneous hours for instance reports writing etc., in the service providing, so as to know the cost of the job to be finished. Of course, there might be other costs as in IT there might be hardware involved and SMEs could just add this with certain profit margin to the job's cost. Through calculating one manpower hour, one could easily control their cost and set their price through a high expense - salary. You might well be able to set discount price as a strategy for your company as well.

The above mentioned topics are from the marketing mix of 4P's as mentioned before during the talks of survival of SMEs and you could find it in the published book mentioned above – price.

Thinking of growth, you might think of promotion as well. Do not go to fairs to promote your businesses as you might not be able to handle too many customers. If you wish to promote your businesses in fairs, firstly you should have already established a venture with other companies local and/or international, if not, stay in local with simple promotion through newspapers or television.

Next stop will be manufacturing industry.

MANUFACTURING INDUSTRY

This is a time to talk about manufacturing industry growth. There are opportunities all over the world through setting booth at fairs for orders all over the world. However, one has to mind the market currency while quoting the orders.

Manufacturing companies might have already hedged foreign exchange through futures and here I would like to say, that under the present downturn economies all over the world, manufacturers can try to add foreign exchange loss to the cost of production in producing products. To calculate this, one can use the Forex futures quote as a basis and calculate the currency gain or loss for cost management. The total cost of the order will have to add in currency loss if there is so to sustain the profit of the company.

Make sure that your company could support extra orders coming through the setting of your booth which is a kind of promotion in a product fair. If you find yourself unable to handle extra orders due to production constraints, do not go for a booth at a fair. Here, innovative production system could be install in the company as Just-in-time (JIT) production system - lowering cost and fasten production will help companies to increase their productivity.

Manufacturing companies could apply for ISO9000: Quality management is to boost up their standard and using quality management to profit more.

Manufacturing companies could set up a retail outlet to sell their products to the market or overseas markets to expand their operations local or international. It can as well be a kind of promotion to the products for orders from clients and can gain profits for both sides through the retail industry expansion strategy by opening a retail outlet.

Another way could gain profits could be establishing warehouse outlet for customers to buy in small quantity or just like having a retail store to sell your products and/or products of clients.

The above is under the 4Ps explained previously and in the published handbook and it is place and promotion strategies used in SMEs for growth.

Next talk will be F&B industry.

F & B INDUSTRY

This is time to talk about F&B industry's growth. The hardest part in F&B industry is pricing. Costing is the topic. I would like to recall the concept of having a computerised accounting system in your company. To price a dish, SMEs should first standardize their orders of recipes. Use gram to standardize your recipes purchase. Having a computerized accounting system, one could see its inventory easily, knowing how recipes go. Then one could know which dish and beverage are the best sell through the sales report. Calculate the cost of each dish is the next step. The amount of recipes used in grammes has to be calculated. One item that had to be calculated into the cost per dish is the salary of a Chef in a minute. Chefs have high salary and one should calculate the cost of a chef in each dish by dividing his salary per minute by the total number of dishes he cooks per minute (estimated cooking time per dish). Electricity expense, water expense, gasoline expense, staff salary and rental expense (if any) should be inserted into costing in minute as well and calculated by dividing these expenses with the total number of dishes per minute and these are major expenses. This is additional cost per dish. Simply add in the recipes cost will know the cost per dish.

Another way to win in costing could be opening another shop. The inventory could be cheaper when ordering in bulks and lessening the cost in the original shop.

Aside from costing, promotion is very important in F&B industry. Try tasting day with your best dishes free of charge for customers to taste is one way.

F&B industry if searching for growth, one could produce dishes served at your site originally to serve in supermarkets or convenient stores. For example, having a Dim Sum set for Chinese restaurants could be a way.

If your business is mature enough for offering franchises, you have to ask for help from marketing companies to help with your franchise and your production of dishes or beverages has to be standardized to sell your franchise. This is a growth development for SMEs and a huge amount of cash has to be paid to marketing firms for marketing your franchise. Make sure that your management and production as well are well developed with which it is the key to franchise success.

I hereby again urge SMEs to set up a computerized accounting system to develop your business with a strong management base for owners.

The next topic will be construction industry.

CONSTRUCTION
INDUSTRY

Let's talk about construction industry. The projects of construction companies will need to be concentrated to grow in projects in a construction company during the growth stage. Construction companies should evaluate the project value to see if it worth to invest in for the businesses. To evaluate a project, one can use Net Present Value analysis to know whether it is worth investing in the project. Net Present value analysis is using the outflow of cash for the project (if any) and estimation of cash inflow for the project over the project years. Each cash flow excluding the initial investment has to multiply PVIF (Present value interest factor) by using the interest rate at the market as return and check the value for PVIF through its table (this is available on the web-site) with the number of years of dealing the project and sum them up. Should the NPV (net present value) calculate as positive take the project and go ahead to invest and if it is negative, do not go for it.

To grow a construction company, one can promote their designers' work for investors. There is architecture design campaign at times. Try to go for a competition and see if the design can be awarded.

Next will be talking about banking industry

BANKING INDUSTRY

Let's talk about banking industry in a SMEs' scenario. If a SME bank wants to grow in their business, they must have excessive cash in hand to reach the target.

To grow, a SME bank has to analyse the needs of its customers firstly. Do their customers want to have convenience from the bank services? What services do its customers want from the bank additional from their present banking services? Probably you will get an answer of phone banking from the customers.

Phone banking is complicated. A Call centre has to be established to meet your service.

Here is a benchmark. A call centre is a cost centre in your bank and you need to know the total cost is from this project. The bench mark of having a call centre in an SME bank is firstly it has to pay for cost for equipment and tools about $3750 per representative in your call centre and salary at around $2300 per representative monthly. A call centre manager is needed and his salary is around $4750 per month. Rental cost of floor space is needed as well. This depends on the size of the call centre.

Establishing one to two branches could be a growth of SMEs banks. This will be a high cost project and SMEs bank has to know whether it is profitable to establish branches for your bank. Establishing branches will help in the maturity stage of SMEs bank and provide other services to customers.

Security service will be an added value to the bank. The bank can provide fingerprints verification system for deposit and cash out procedures with photos in the bank database at the time of opening a bank account and Bank book should have photos of the owner for security and fraud activities.

I hereby suggest SME bank does not go for Investment banking for generation of profits as well as providing additional service to its customers. The main reason is that SME bank might not be able to compete with large bank with investment service as well as investment bank and does not cover up the cost for the setting up of investment banking in SME bank. I suggest SME bank goes for investment banking in their maturity stage for sustainability purposes.

Next talk will be hotel industry.

HOTEL INDUSTRY

This is a piece for hotel industry. For growth of SMEs hotel, SMEs hotel can search for higher rating stars in the hotel. There is international organization and entities rating hotels in different countries and SMEs hotel can grow by increasing the service of the hotel through several aspects. SMEs hotel can have a glance below to see how to rate oneself to higher star hotel. I heard from an hotelier that a Grand Piano can get higher hotel rating star. Below is a standard for SMEs hotel reference.

Hotel star		Excerpt of the catalogue of criteria
★	Tourist	<ul><li>100% of the rooms with shower/WC or bath tub/WC</li><li>Daily room cleaning</li><li>100% of the rooms with color-TV together with remote control</li><li>Table and chair</li><li>Soap or body wash</li><li>Reception service</li><li>Facsimile at the reception</li><li>Publicly available telephone for guests</li><li>Extended breakfast</li><li>Beverage offer in the hotel</li><li>Deposit possibility</li></ul>

★S	*Superior Tourist*	The Superior flag is provided when the additional service and accommodation provisions are not sufficient for the next Hotel star. The bathroom facilities are usually at the same level as for two stars hotels but built from cheaper materials. The cost for regular inspection by independent associations is waived as well.
★★	*Standard*	In addition to the single star (*) hotels: - Breakfast buffet - Reading light next to the bed - Bath essence or shower gel - Bath towels - Linen shelves - Offer of sanitary products (e.g. toothbrush, toothpaste, shaving kit) - Credit Cards
★★S	*Superior Standard*	The Superior flag is provided when the additional service and accommodation provisions are not sufficient for the next Hotel star. The Standard-Superior does usually offer the same service level as three-star hotels but the interiors of the hotel are smaller and cheaper so that the three stars were not to be awarded by the inspection body. A two-star superior does not require

		mystery guesting.
★★★	Comfort	In addition to the standard star (**) hotels: • Reception opened 14 hours, accessible by phone 24 hours from inside and outside, bilingual staff (e.g. German/English) • Three piece suite at the reception, luggage service • Beverage offer in the room • Telephone in the room • Internet access in the room or in the public area • Heating facility in the bathroom, hair-dryer, cleansing tissue • Dressing mirror, place to put the luggage/suitcase • Sewing kit, shoe polish utensils, laundry and ironing service • Additional pillow and additional blanket on demand • Systematic complaint management system
★★★S	Superior Comfort	The Superior flag is provided when the additional service and accommodation

		provisions are not sufficient for the next Hotel star. The accommodation facilities for a superior hotel need to be on a modern level and fully renovated which is checked regularly.
★★★★	First Class	In addition to the comfort star (***) hotels: - Reception opened 18 hours, accessible by phone 24 hours from inside and outside - Lobby with seats and beverage service - Breakfast buffet or breakfast menu card via room service - Minibar or 24 hours beverages via room service - Upholstered chair/couch with side table - Bath robe and slippers on demand - Cosmetic products (e.g. shower cap, nail file, cotton swabs), vanity mirror, tray of a large scale in the bathroom) - Internet access and internet terminal - "À la carte"-restaurant
★★★★S	First Class	The Superior flag is provided when the first class hotel has a proven high quality not only

		Superior	in the rooms. The superior hotels provide for additional facilities in the hotel like a sauna or a workout room. The quality is checked regularly by mystery guesting of an external inspection service.
★★★★★		Luxury	In addition to the first class (****) hotels: - Reception opened 24 hours, multilingual staff - Doorman-service or valet parking - Concierge, page boy - Spacious reception hall with several seats and beverage service - Personalized greeting for each guest with fresh flowers or a present in the room - Minibar and food and beverage offer via room service during 24 hours - Personal care products in flacons - Internet-PC in the room - Safe in the room - Ironing service (return within 1 hour), shoe polish service - Turndown service in the evening

			• Mystery guesting
★★★★★S		Superior Luxury	The Luxury star hotels need to attain high expectations of an international guest service. The Superior Luxury star is only awarded with a system of intensive guest care.

- From www.wikipedia.org

What is the use of having higher star in SMEs hotel? The rate of the room will increase with increase in service and provided luxurious service to their customers. Renovation could through increasing higher star as a choice as well but this place a high cost recover for SMEs hotel.

Another one is having small items that could promote your hotel. Towels and Amenities with printed logo could increase your service grade to in house guests and that if your towels are high quality, customers can buy for example for souvenirs or self use. Amenities could be souvenirs too. I here suggest through of having a facial mask as amenities for both male and female relaxation in their rooms at your hotel as amenities can be a plus in your service.

The marketing department of a SMEs hotel could be set up for growth of banquets and room sales. SMEs hotel just need to hire a Director of Marketing and two more marketing staffs could SMEs hotel start searching for business opportunities. This includes a PR manager of SMEs hotel producing advertisement and pamphlets to help out search of customers and the exposure of the SMEs hotel.

Make sure you have enough rooms for sale if not cross sell to other nearby SMEs hotel if there is any.

Next will be academic institution.

ACADEMIC INSTITUTION

Here comes a piece for academic Institutions. I hereby refer to education centre which are SMEs to develop into a university if there could be high investment on it.

Education Centres are SMEs which offered courses to customers like diplomas and certificates. For growth, there could be area of expansion by having distance learning courses. However, technology is a big cost for distance learning depending on which kind of distance learning the education centre is affordable.

There are two types of distance learning technology. One is namely synchronous learning and the other is namely asynchronous learning. Synchronous learning had to import technology like web-conferencing, videoconferencing, educational TV, instructional TV etc. which are high cost. With asynchronous learning, there are e-mails, message board forum, video and audio recording, fax and print materials and it is lower cost for the growth of SMEs.

SMEs education centre can try to sell distance learning degree programme of universities for growth by collaborating with universities. Advertisement and a course consultant would be needed to develop this strategy.

For growth, SMEs education centre can diversify its originally offered courses to other fields. If your courses are mainly targeting in business administration, try to diversify them to social science or technology to attract different customers for your courses.

There is substantial competition in distance learning in education centre. To run out of the competition, you can build up your brand name with services offered to customers. Advertisement for your brand name is then necessary. You can have value-added services to customers for example funding programme linking with banks offered to customers to take courses in your centre for example, for a degree programme.

For a wild thought, education centre can seek for opportunities to grow into a mid-size university. Angel financing could be a way for you to grow. The campus is a strong asset for the education centre. Seek for investors to build up your campus for growth of your business.

This is the end of this handbook and I am looking forward to introduce another one in the near future.

Reference:

www.wikipedia.com

Owens M. *Funds needed for setting up a call centre.* eHow Contributor.

Gitman, J.L., (2009). *Principles of Managerial Finance*. Boston, MA: Pearson Education.

www.ingramcontent.com/pod-product-compliance
Lightning Source LLC
Chambersburg PA
CBHW061521180526
45171CB00001B/286